Famous Type Faces

Tara Asadi

Published by: Top Ten Award International Network
Vancouver, BC **CANADA**
Email: Info@toptenaward.net
www.toptenaward.net

Ordering Information: Quantity sales. Special discounts are available on quantity purchases by universities, schools, corporations, associations, and others. For details, contact the "Sales Department" at the above mentioned email address.
Famous Type Faces/T.Asadi—1st ed.

ISBN: 978-1-990451-11-9

I dedicate this book to my dearest family, as well as my best friends: Deon and Phia.

Table of Contents

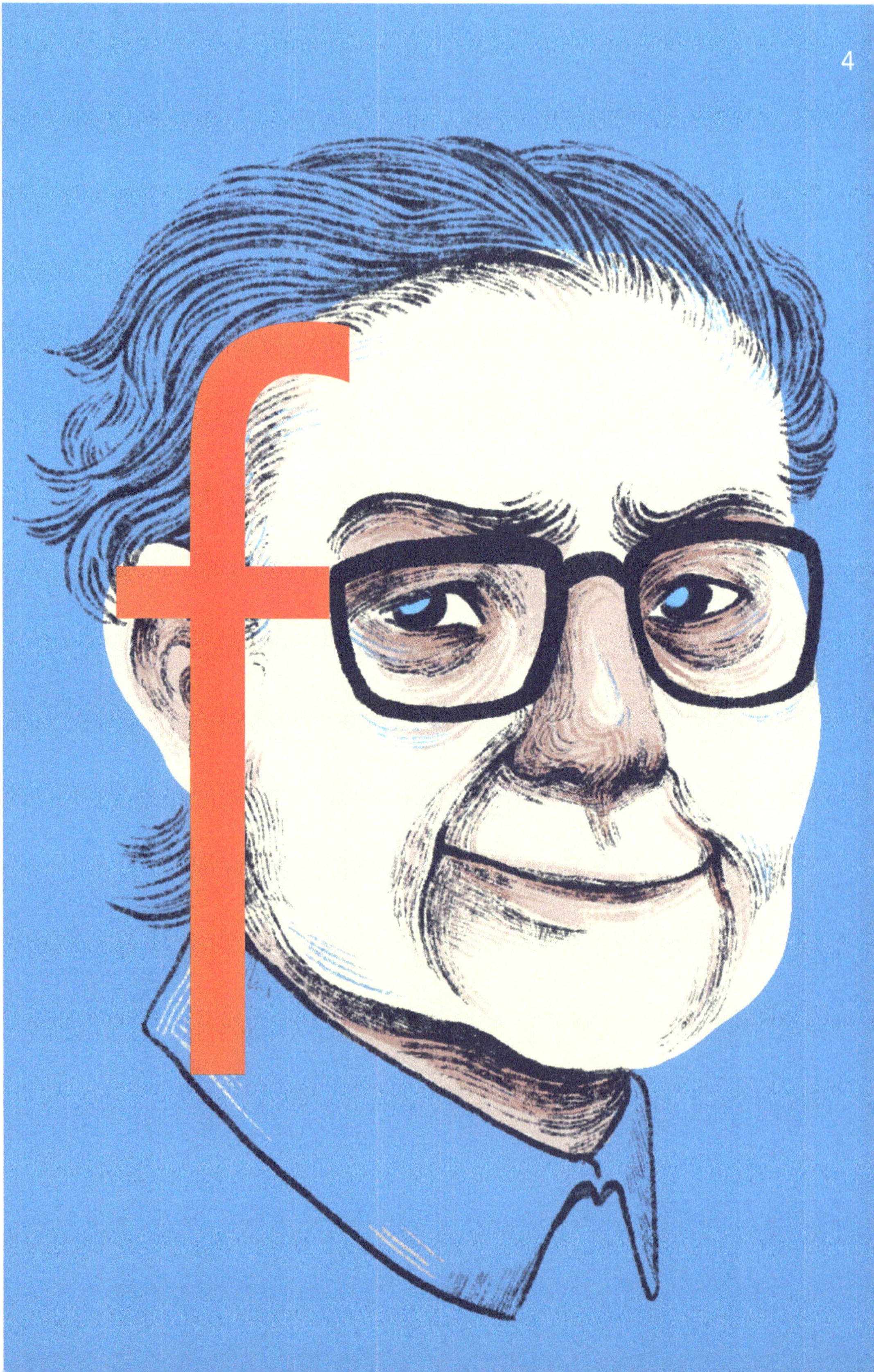

Frutiger

Adrian Frutiger

1928 – 2015

Adrian Frutiger was one of the most influential type designers in typographic history. Adrian was originally born in 1928 Switzerland and as he grew up so did his admiration for letterforms. Alongside his early experimentation with handwriting and penmanship, he developed a love of sculpture that unfortunately was disapproved of by the adult role models in his life. However, that did not deter him from incorporating his knowledge of sculpture into his type designs. Which led him to landing successful careers later on, the first of which being under a French type foundry. Later on, he would move on to create typefaces for the French community and where he would develop a font named after himself.

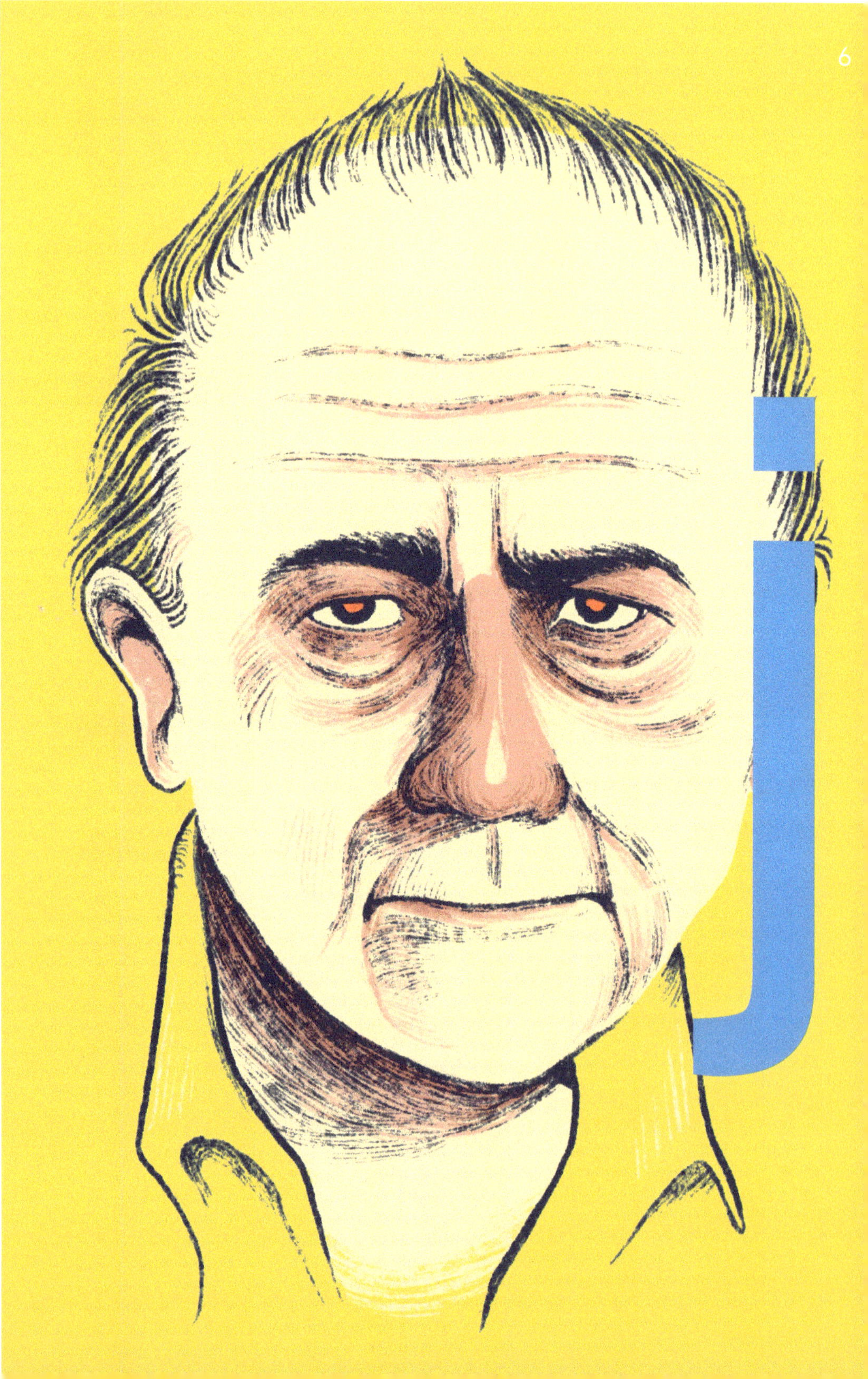

Helvetica

Max Miedinger

1910 – 1980

Max Miedinger was the creator of one of the most versatile fonts in the history of typography. This typeface has withstood the test of time since it was first introduced in 1957. Max was born in Zurich, Switzerland in 1910. From a young age, he was urged to enter the visual design world and was taught the way of type as he grew older. He finished his training in the late 1930's and went on to be hired as a typographer under Globus in 1936. What happened after he moved on from Globus was his kickstart to fame, the creation of Helvetica. Its origins began back in 1956, with a commission from Eduard Hoffman, a director of the Haas Type Foundry, who commissioned Max to develop a brand-new sans-serif type face.

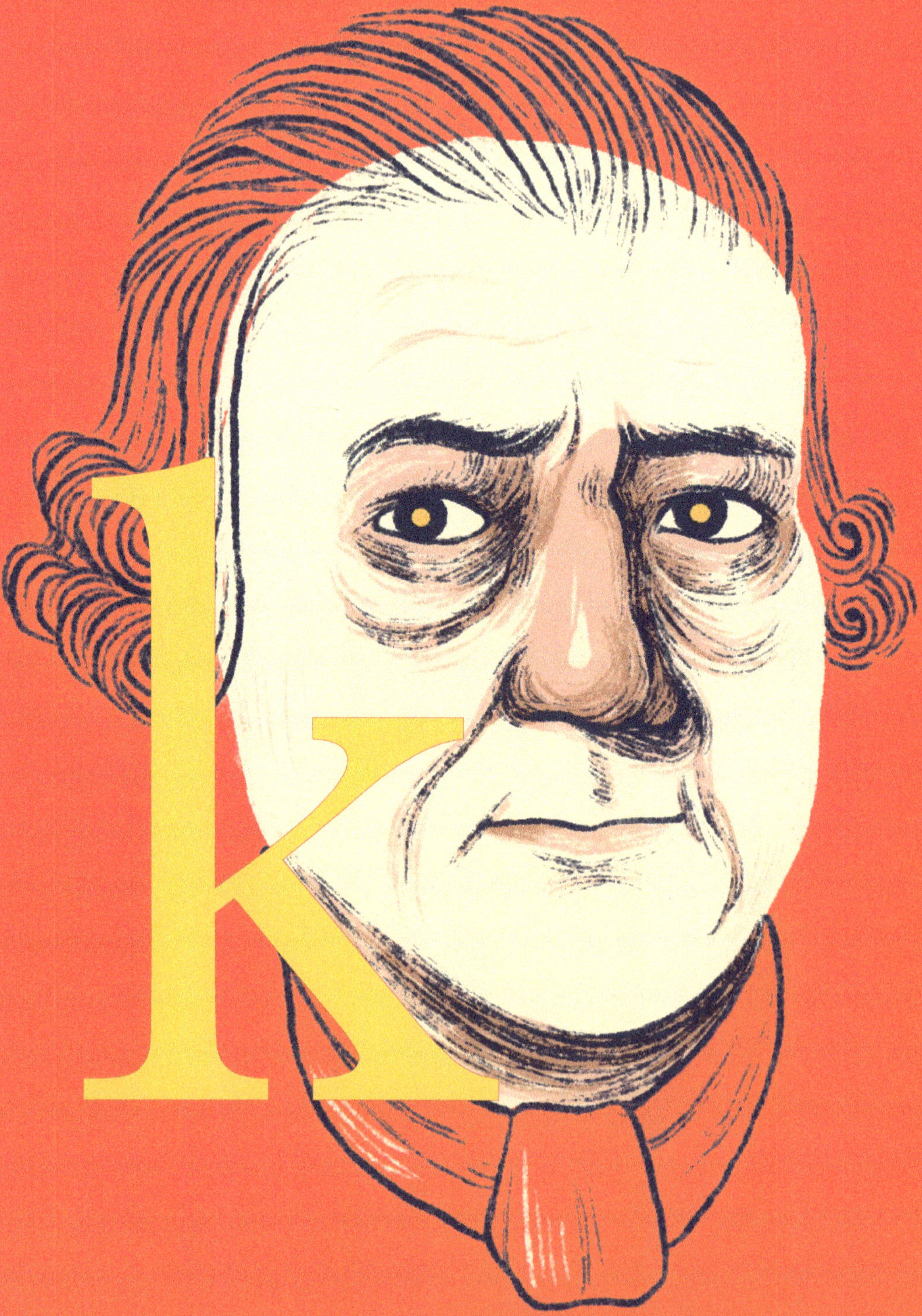
k

Baskerville

John Baskerville

1706 – 1775

John Baskerville was arguably the first revolutionary that sparked the interest of more modern serifs. John originally started a varnishing business instead of a press foundry however, this was a deliberate choice by him so that he could use the funds from that business to experiment with type. He would then take on to print his own renditions of books, the Bible being his proudest achievement. Despite his success in publishing, his approach to type design was a little too radical for the English population back then which led to him being rejected for his prints. The font Baskerville came to being after his death. Since his death, his works have been revised and his fonts were updated for general use.

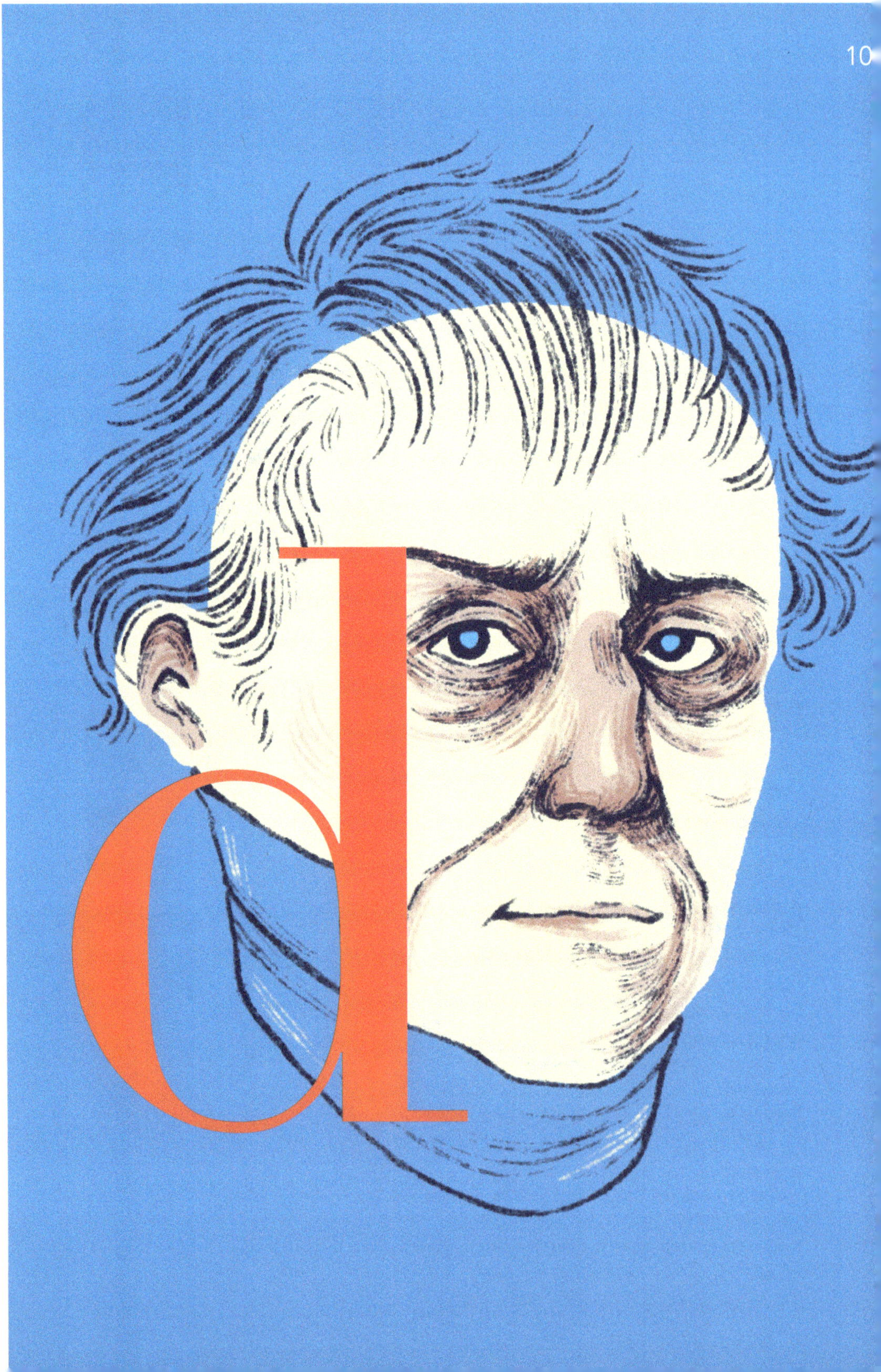
d

Didot

Firmin Didot

1784 – 1811

Firmin Didot was part of a type revolution, as well as the French Revolution, that paved the way for more modern typefaces. Firmin's destiny was sealed when he was born into a family of printers. Thus, from a young age, he had lots of exposure to typesetting and print. In 1795, he became renowned for the accuracy and affordability of his work. He even got a director spot in Napoleon's imperial type foundry. Alongside Giambattista Bodoni, he sprouts to life a new serif typeface that was swaying with elegance. While creating Didot, he was heavily inspired by John Baskerville's approach to type, which was to diverge from the old-style print and into more legible prints with separate letters. Didot has become a font-family of its own.

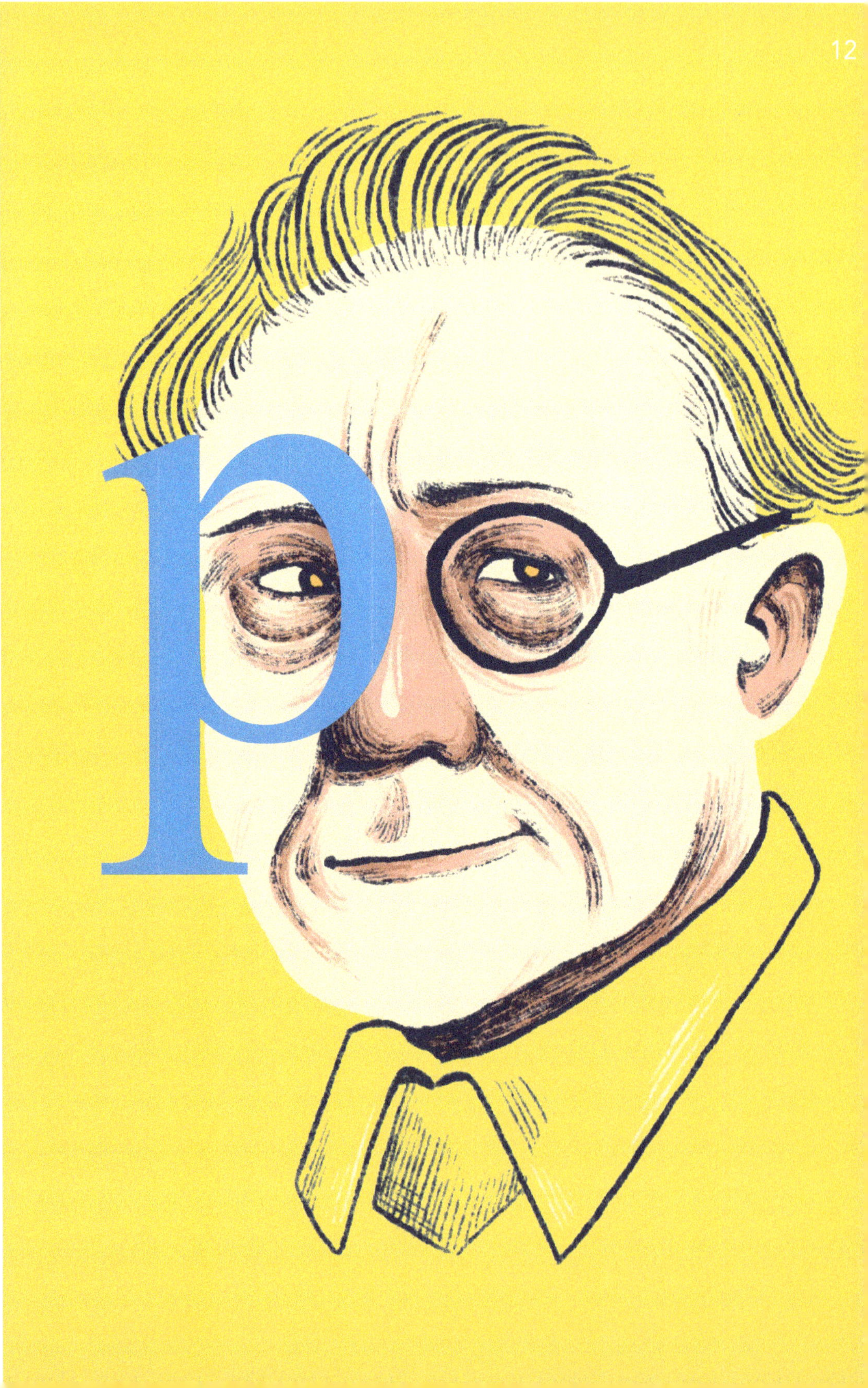

Times New Roman

Stanley Morrison

1889 – 1967

Stanley Morison was creator of the typeface most adored by many school teachers. He had originally spent his working career as a Clerk in London but, after a twist of fate, he came across newspaper from the Times in 1912 that sparked his interest in typepography. He would then go on to study and pursue learning more about typesetting. He became a master of writing and type as he was offered more opportunities until he went on to develop a hot-new serif typeface called Times New Roman. As fate would have it, he became a part of the Times newspaper staff in 1929, and that's where Times New Roman's story begun. The font, due to its legibility in publications, became one of the best fonts for worksheets!

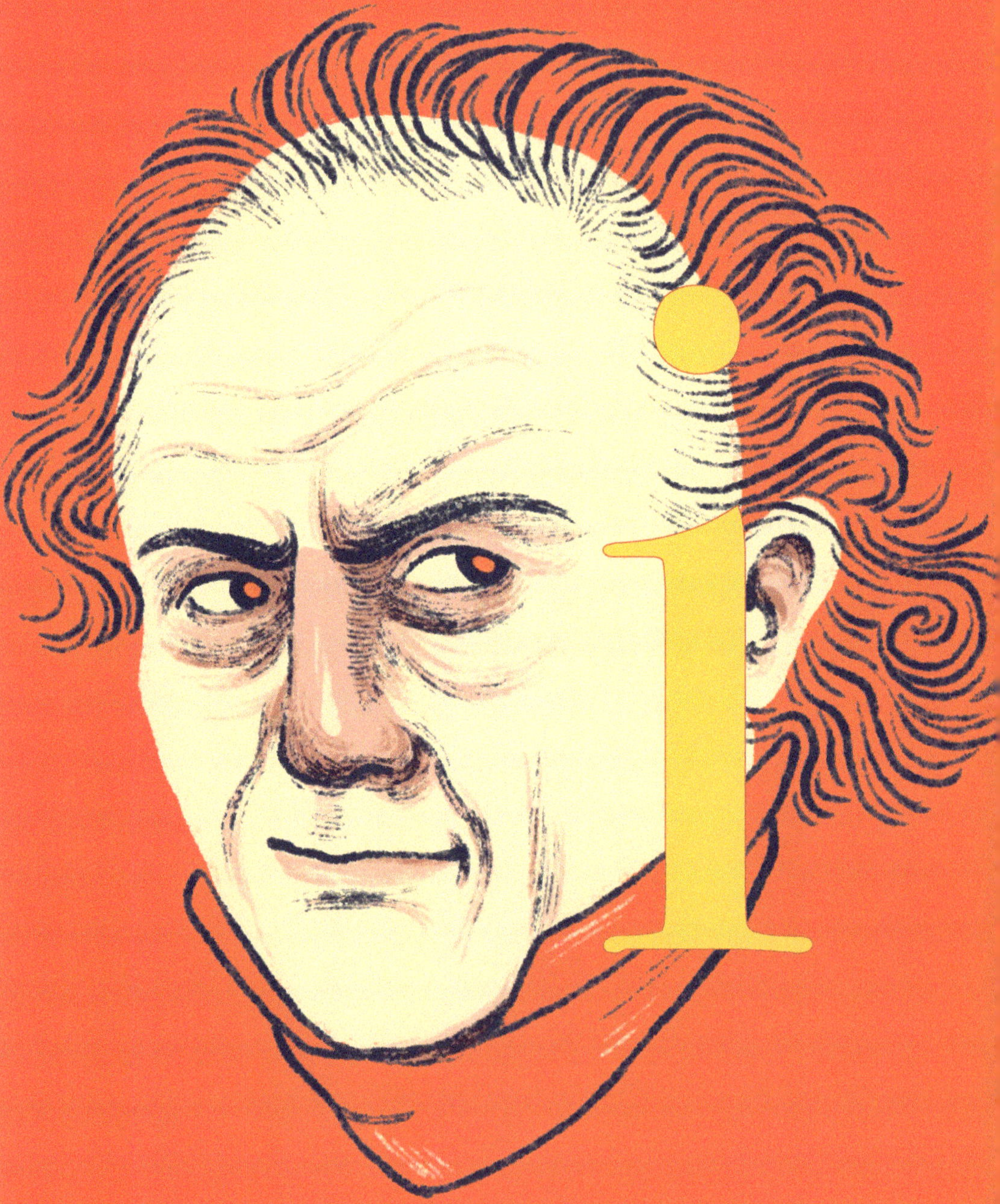

Bodoni

Giambattista Bodoni

1740 – 1813

Giambattista Bodoni, alongside Firmin Didot, participated in the type revolution that modernized serif fonts. Giambattista was also born into a family of printing blood and went on to Rome to take up an apprenticeship at a press foundry under the Roman Catholic Church. He was taken into the Royal press in which he printed books in Italian, Latin and Greek. Giambattista originally favored the decorative old-style but then warmed up to the modern theories that were surfacing. So much so that he later fully abandoned the intricacy of the old-style for a completely simple modern style.Many of the common fonts we see today are part of the Bodoni family and a testament to how modern is modern serifs were.

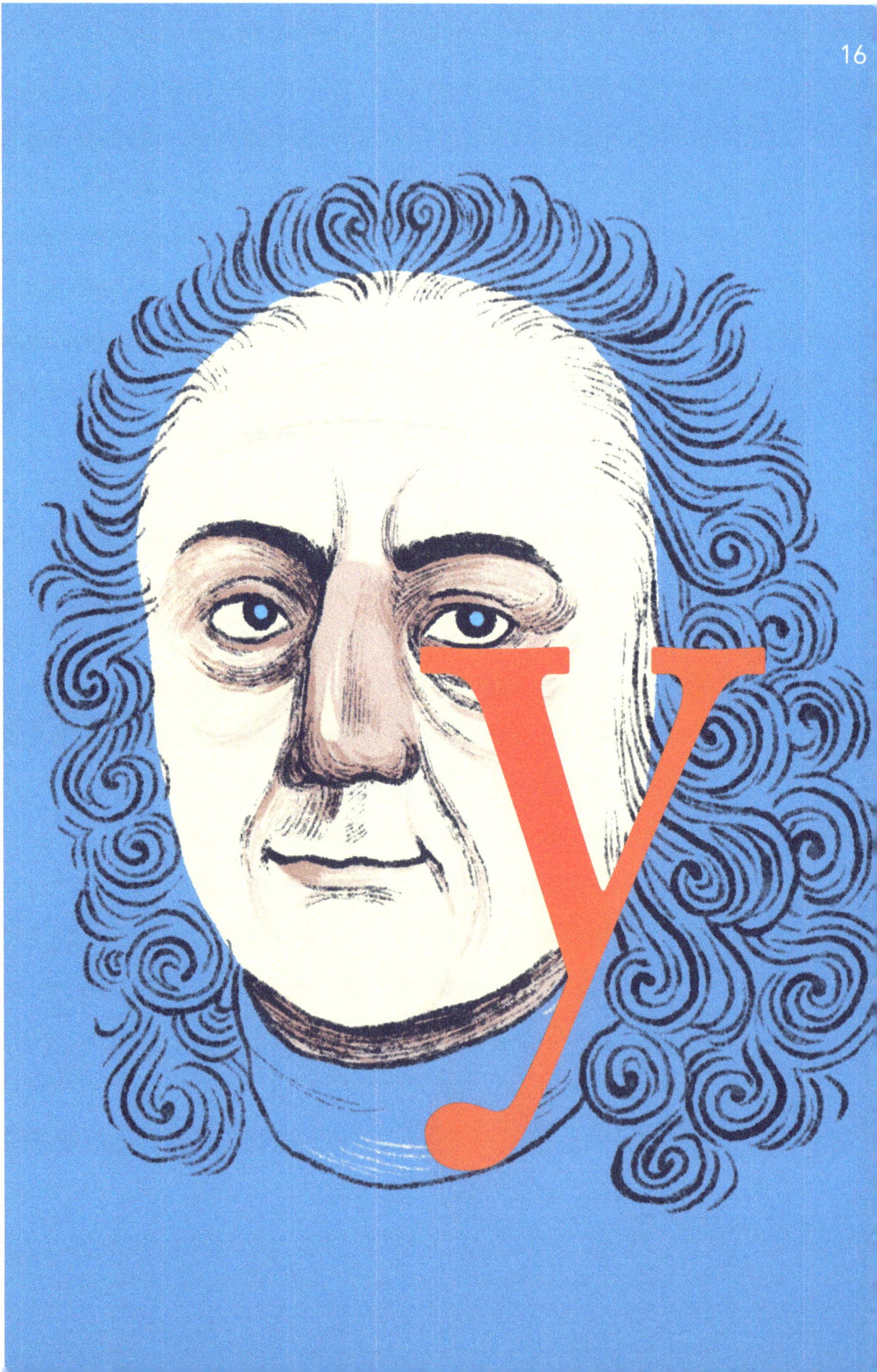

Caslon

William Caslon

1692 – 1766

William Caslon is an iconic British type founder that helped with modernizing books and book publishing. His origins began with being an apprentice for an engraver of gunlocks and barrels. This led him to establishing his own engraving shop later on. While doing so, he became fascinated with book binding and printing which resulted in his deeper exploration of typography. Through that William would go on to create Caslon, an elegantly legible font, that ended up being an English favorite. His typeface would then go on to travel across the globe and continue to be relevant in the future.

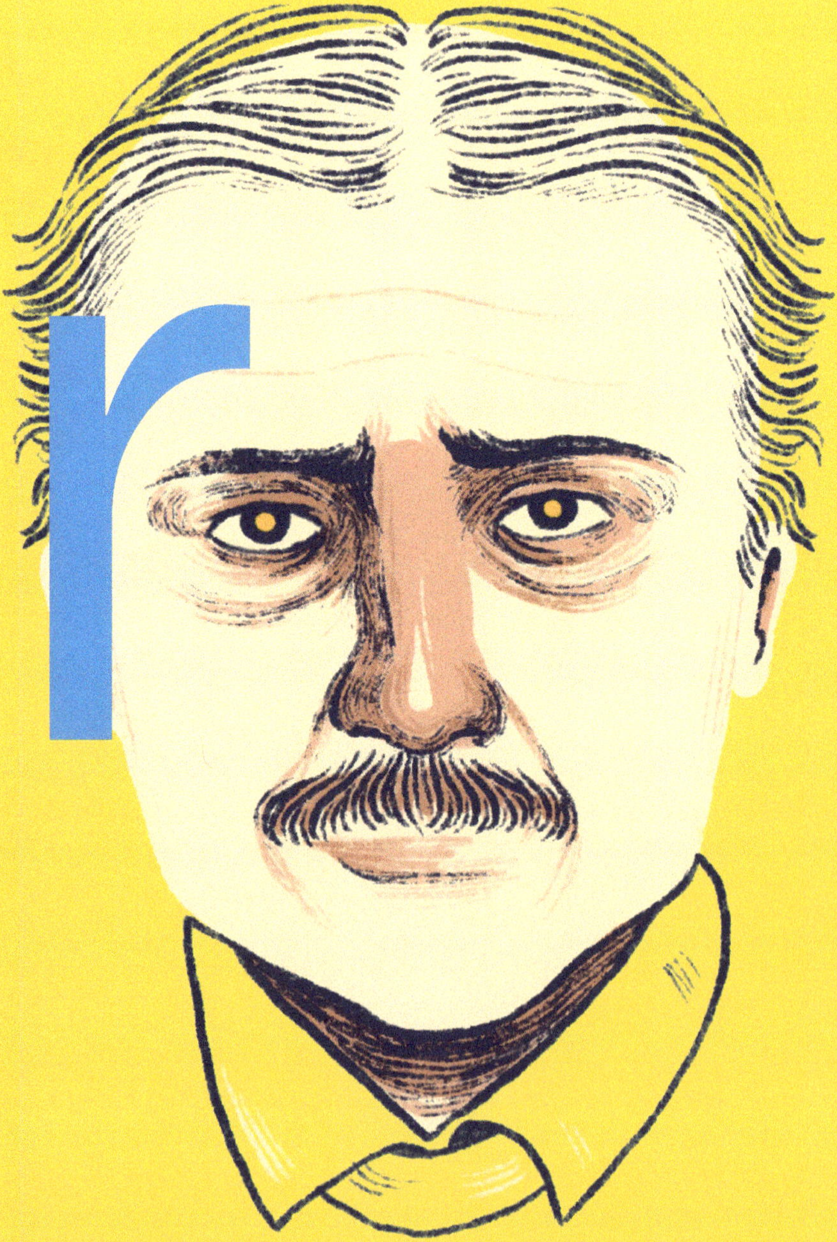

Franklin Gothic

Morris Fuller Benton

1872 – 1948

Morris Fuller Benton was known for being chalk full of fresh ideas of typography. He was born in New Jersey, to a type founder father that would later inspire Morris to walk down that same path. He would grow up helping his parent and develop a passion for fonts and print. As his eagerness to step foot into the industry took hold, he would go on to have a smooth education and slide into the print industry to work alongside his father. His determination showed in production as he would create over 200 various font-families, all of which being uniquely different from one another. One which was Franklin Gothic.

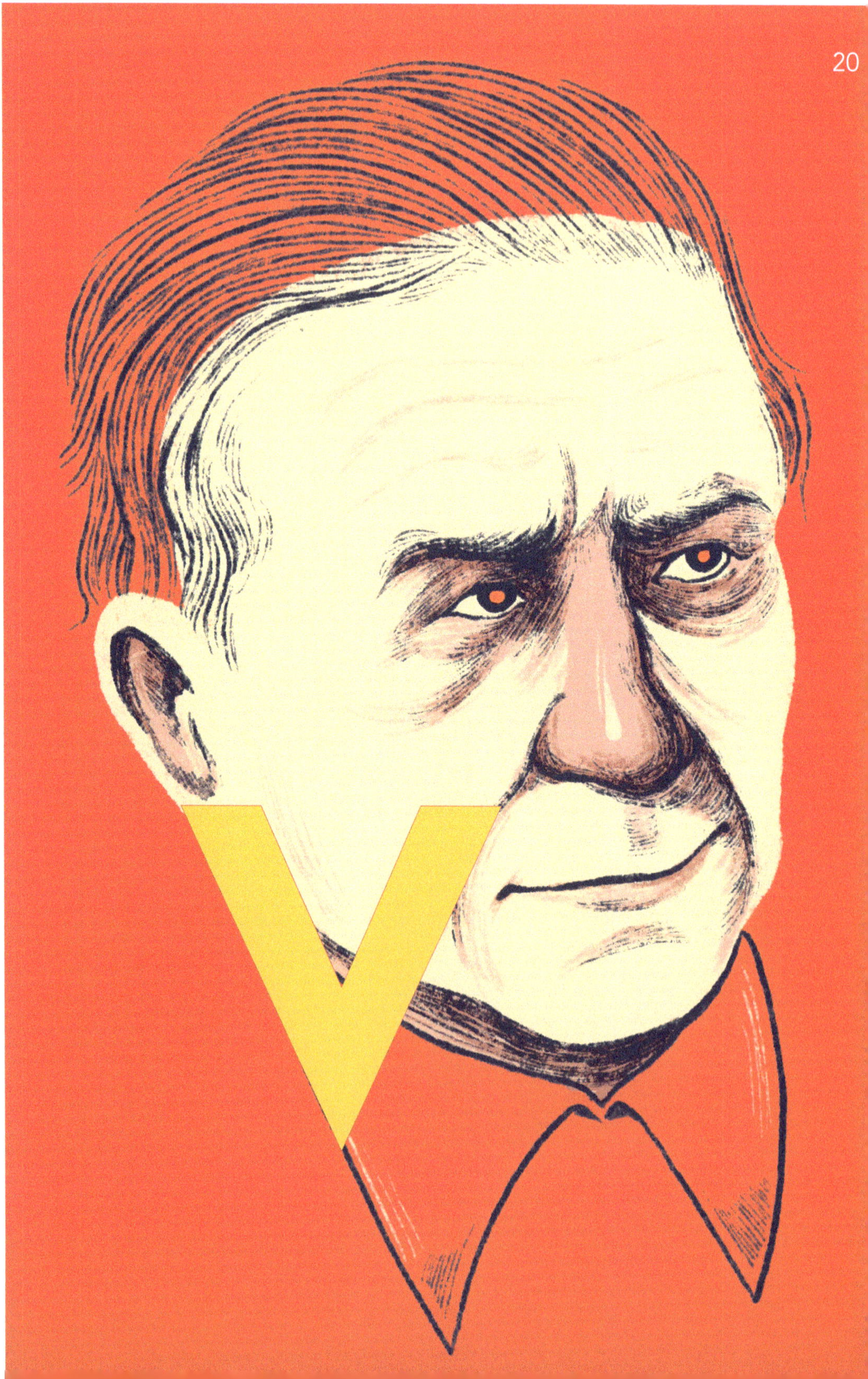

Futura

Paul Renner

1878 – 1956

Paul Renner was an influential painter, designer and teacher that would develop one of the most used fonts in modern day. While originally favoring traditional mediums and art, after attending a conference full of talented creatives, his perspective changed. He began to pursue a more graphic and geometrical approach. With this newfound inspiration, Paul would go on to create sans-serif typefaces, one of which being Futura. Development on the font would begin in 1924, however, due to the rising political climate in Germany at the time, he wouldn't be able to finish his masterpiece until 3 years after.

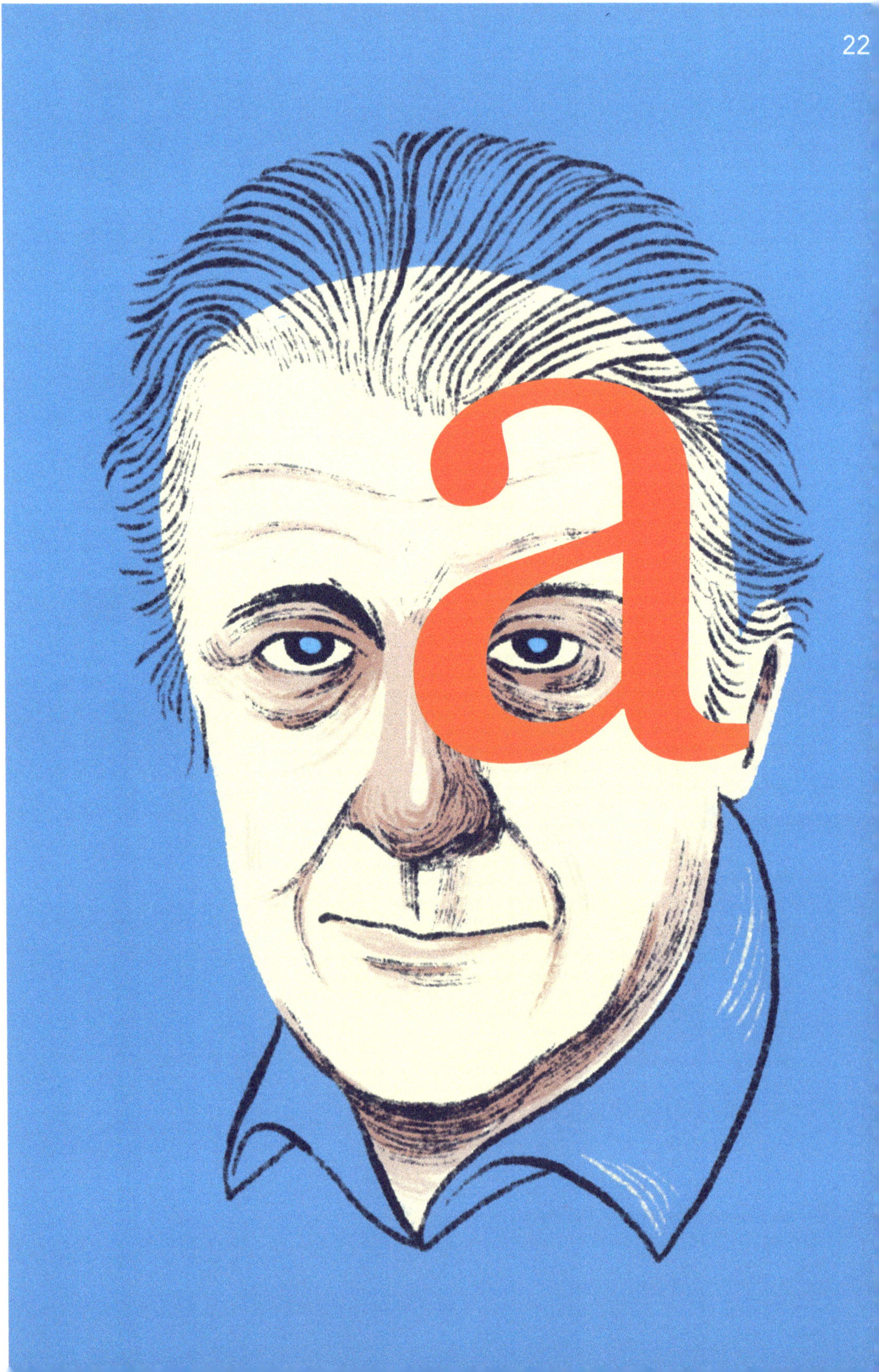
a

Georgia

Matthew Carter

1937 – Present

Matthew Carter is the British type designer that improved typography on the computer. He has 50 years of experience under his belt as well as his own type foundry, known as Carter and Cone Type Inc.. He is an influential typographer that shares his journey with the world by participating in public events, such as TEDx. One of the most pivotal moments in his career was when he was commissioned by Microsoft to create screen-friendly fonts. One of the fruits of Matthew's labor was the font Georgia, which is a legible serif font and one that continues to be used throughout the web.

Bibliography:

"Adrian Frutiger: Biography, Designs and Facts." *Famous Graphic Designers*, https://www.famousgraphicdesigners.org/adrian-frutiger.

"Giambattista Bodoni." *Encyclopædia Britannica*, Encyclopædia Britannica, Inc., https://www.britannica.com/biography/Giambattista-Bodoni.

"John Baskerville." *Encyclopædia Britannica*, Encyclopædia Britannica, Inc., https://www.britannica.com/biography/John-Baskerville.

"Matthew Carter." *FontShop*, https://www.fontshop.com/designers/matthew-carter.

"Matthew Carter." *FontShop*, https://www.fontshop.com/designers/matthew-carter.

Monotype GmbH, info@linotype.com. "Morris Fuller Benton." *Morris Fuller Benton - Linotype Font Feature*, https://www.linotype.com/3525/morris-fuller-benton.html.

Monotype GmbH, info@linotype.com. "Font Designer – Max Miedinger." *Max Miedinger - Font Designer of Helvetica*, https://www.linotype.com/522/max-miedinger.html.

"Morris Fuller Benton." *Identifont*, http://www.identifont.com/show?16W.

"Paul Renner (1878-1956)." *Paul Renner*, https://www2.palomar.edu/users/gkelley/PaulRenner.html.

"Paul Renner: Biography, Designs and Facts." *Famous Graphic Designers*, https://www.famousgraphicdesigners.org/paul-renner.

"Stanley Morison." *Encyclopædia Britannica*, Encyclopædia Britannica, Inc., https://www.britannica.com/biography/Stanley-Morison.

TypeRoom. "Firmin Didot: 10 Things to Know About." *TypeRoom*, https://www.typeroom.eu/firmin-didot-10-things-to-know-about.

"William Caslon." *Encyclopædia Britannica*, Encyclopædia Britannica, Inc., https://www.britannica.com/biography/William-Caslon.

www.ingramcontent.com/pod-product-compliance
Ingram Content Group UK Ltd.
Pitfield, Milton Keynes, MK11 3LW, UK
UKHW060116010826
14089UKWH00003B/19

9 781990 451119